CALLED OUT

FRATERNITIES AND SORORITIES: HOW TO GET OUT OF SOMETHING YOU SHOULD HAVE NEVER BEEN IN

PORCHIA CARTER

Copyright © 2023 Porchia Carter

All rights reserved. No part of this publication may be reproduced, distributed, or transmitted in any form or by any means, including photocopying, recording, or other electronic or mechanical methods, without the prior written permission of the publisher, except in the case of brief quotations embodied in critical reviews and certain other noncommercial uses permitted by copyright law.

Scripture Quotations:

Scriptures marked NKJV are taken from the **NEW KING JAMES VERSION (NKJV)**. Scripture taken from the NEW KING JAMES VERSION®. Copyright© 1982 by Thomas Nelson, Inc. Used by permission. All rights reserved.

Disclaimer:

This book describes occurrences in the life of Porchia Carter according to the author's memory and perspective. All of the stories are her truths. However, some names and identifying details have been changed to keep the privacy of those involved.

ISBN: 979-8-218-30486-7

DEDICATION

This book is dedicated to Jesus Christ.

Thank You Lord for making me free.

DEDICATION.

This book is dedicated to Jesus Christ,
Through Whose love it could be written.

CONTENTS

DEDICATION iii

INTRODUCTION 1
Is God Calling You Out? 1

1 HOW IT STARTED 5
The Identity Crisis 5

2 HOW IT ENDED 17
It Is That Deep 17

3 HOW TO GET FREE 33
Breaking Evil Covenants 33

4 HOW TO NAVIGATE THE TRANSITION 73
Please God, Not People 73

5 HOW TO FIGHT THIS FIGHT 83
Self Defense VS God's Defense 83

CONCLUSION 89
True Identity in Christ 89

ACKNOWLEDGEMENTS 93

ABOUT THE AUTHOR 95

INTRODUCTION

Is God Calling You Out?

When God calls you out of something you thought would be a lifelong commitment, it feels like ripping apart extremely tight velcro. That's precisely how it felt when God called me out of Delta Sigma Theta Sorority Inc. (Delta). I had a tough time leaving because I had pledged my lifetime commitment to the sorority, as the Delta intake books recommended. I also didn't see anything wrong with it. I wasn't ready to give up my connections and everything I had gained as a member of the organization. I had plans to make it a legendary legacy for myself and future generations. However, I had no idea how detrimental that decision was to my life.

Before I take you through my journey from start to finish, let me define what a sorority is. A sorority is a social organization comprised of women who share similar values, with a goal to build sisterhood while contributing to the betterment of communities around the country.

These sororities are often joined by undergraduate women on college campuses, but there are also graduate chapters that initiate women in grad school. Delta just so happens to be a part of the "Divine Nine," which is a collective of Black Greek Letter Organizations (BGLOs) made up of fraternities and sororities that promote leadership, scholarship, and community service within the Black community. These fraternities and sororities are also known as secret societies.

This is the first book in the "Called Out" series. I chose to begin with this topic because it was the first thing God ever called me out of that I had a hard time with. I didn't quite understand all of the spiritual implications of being a member of a secret society. I felt like because I didn't idolize the organization, my faith was fine. I had no issues and no worries. It wasn't until I decided to go deeper with God that I realized I had been deceived.

This book is intended for a diverse audience. It is for those who have welcomed the Lord and Savior Jesus Christ into their hearts while also holding memberships in secret societies. It is for individuals who believe in Jesus Christ and are contemplating joining such societies. It is for those currently involved in secret societies who may one day come to know Jesus Christ as their savior. Additionally, it is for any believer in Jesus Christ who has friends, family members, or loved ones within secret societies and yearns to discover the truth. Lastly, this book is for anyone seeking to elevate their walk with Jesus Christ beyond the confines of societal norms.

As believers in Jesus Christ, should we be members of secret societies? Should we pledge our love and loyalty to fraternities and sororities? Should we ever prioritize "good things" over godly things? These are some of the questions we, as believers, should consistently ask ourselves when exploring this topic. It is my prayer that these questions get answered for you as you read this book.

1

HOW IT STARTED

The Identity Crisis

Being willing to put your life on the line for something just to fit in seems crazy until you're the one doing it. I was not fully aware of my identity in Christ when I made the decision to join Delta Sigma Theta Sorority Inc. I thought I knew God because I grew up in church, however, my behaviors in college showed something different. When you truly know God, and have a relationship with Him, then you know more about yourself because we are made in His image and likeness. My lack of understanding who I was led me to try finding it in other people, places and things. One of those things was Delta.

I first learned of Delta by talking to a friend during my senior year of high school. This friend of mine used to watch their videos and research their website during breaks in one of our classes. I remember asking her what she was into, and she explained that it was a sorority she planned to join when she got to college. I thought it was cool, but I wasn't interested until I got to my college campus and saw them on the yard. At that point, I was highly intrigued.

These delta women weren't regular women. They were bold, lively, fierce, and demanded the attention of everyone in any room they walked into. They were creative and had the best events out of all the organizations on campus. Delta week was better than SEC (Student Elections Commissions) week when the campaigners running for student government offices would try to solicit votes from students. In my opinion, they were unmatched by any other organization on campus at that time. I wanted that same status. I aspired to carry myself with their fearlessness and dignity. I desired the very characteristics I saw in them, not even realizing that I already possessed them. I wanted people to look at me with the same reverence and respect that they afforded to the Deltas on campus.

By the time my sophomore year of college arrived, I was already involved in numerous campus organizations, leaving little room to join Delta. My desire to become a part of it waned a bit. I was deeply focused on my Media Leadership and Performance track in Mass Comm. I served as the operations manager of the campus radio station, produced at least two shows, acted as one of the head news anchors for our news program, was part of a dance organization, a member of the National Association of Colored Women's Clubs, and I even had a minor in Spanish. I was also planning to apply for a summer study abroad program in Costa Rica. I had no business trying to squeeze pledging into my schedule, but curiosity got the best of me.

I was on the phone with my friend from high school one day when she brought up Delta to me again. She had been talking about it since high school, so I knew she was going to do it. She mentioned the Rush (delta interest meeting) for her campus was coming up and, I should see when it was happening on my campus. I began to ask around.

I had quite a few friends who wanted to be Deltas, and they always talked about it. They shared so much information with me. One of them warned me that I didn't want to be on that "train" with them, and should wait until my junior year. Other friends encouraged me because they wanted me to be their line sister. I even fasted and prayed with a few of them to make the line with them (lol). I laugh at that now because what was I thinking, and what were we really doing?

One of my friends told me I needed to find someone who was already a Delta to express my interest to because a lot of them were already on "pre-line." Pre-line was the underground line made up of girls who desired to be Deltas, and had already started making calls to existing Deltas, and doing things for them before the official invitation was sent out. My friends told me I had a better chance of joining if I was on "pre-line".

When I found the person I wanted to express interest to, I told her that I wanted to "talk." She pulled me outside and said, "Porchia I already know what you want to ask me, and this ain't what you want." She then told me to focus on my major and my career goals that she knew I had, and keep it moving. I walked away from that conversation feeling bad that I had no connection to join "pre-line" instead of listening to her advice.

Turns out I had all of the qualifications needed to make the line when Rush came around. I was considered a "must have". At that time, I had a 3.6 GPA, the right amount of community service hours, experience being a part of other organizations, and I had the Delta advisor on campus to write my entry letter. Going to Rush was an eye-opening experience for me. I only wanted to be a delta at that time because of what I saw from the current Deltas on campus. However, at Rush, they began to explain the sisterhood, scholarship and service portion of the organization, which had me hooked to learn more.

They shared stories of their initiatives that had positively impacted the Black community, their achievements in promoting academic excellence worldwide, and their various programs aimed at improving education, political awareness, health, and more. All the information I received was incredibly inspiring. I believed this was something worth being a part of. They even emphasized that the organization was founded on "Christian Principles." Although I was lukewarm in my faith at that time, I took my faith seriously because I had grown up in the church. Anything labeled "Christian" meant that God wanted me to be a part of it.

After all of the interviews, letters, signatures, and intake money of a thousand dollars, I had officially made the line. The night I found out I made it was when I found out the organization was not so Christian. Christian women aren't supposed to treat each other with this kind of treatment. Over the next month or so, I underwent experiences that I wouldn't wish upon anyone. I couldn't even imagine allowing my daughter to partake in some of the things these women did to me. However, it was the process of being "Made" into a Delta woman. In Delta, if you are "Made" it is worn as a badge of honor. It means that you didn't just attend the pyramid classes, pass the intake tests, do the rituals, and sign the papers at the initiation ceremony. Instead, you pledged to the sorority with your blood, sweat, and tears. That is exactly what I did.

The night of our acceptance into the pledging process, they called each of us and had us meet at an apartment. They instructed us to turn off the location sharing on our phones and keep them off until we officially became Deltas. They introduced us to the "Dean of Pledges" (DP) and the Assistant Dean of Pledges (ADP), who would lead our underground process. They were different from the Minerva Circle women, the committee responsible for planning and administering the activities of the Membership Intake Program. We had to answer to the Minerva Circle during the day and the DP and ADP at night.

The DP and ADP gave us all the instructions we needed for "Set." There was money that needed to be collected. We had to purchase all-black uniforms that we wore every night. We had to get location details for nightly meetups. We had to make arrangements and create assignments for so many things because we would now be living together for the majority of this pledge process. We even had to collect contact information for every single prophyte (women from previous lines who crossed before us) because we had to call them every day. All of this had to be done for "set."

"Set" was where we met with prophytes each night to be "made" into delta women. It is where they tested our knowledge of the information learned in PPP class as well as information we were supposed to know about that specific chapter and its members. In "set" they made us line up with our heads back as far as possible while being ready to pop them back up every time we mentioned the name delta. They often made us scoot across the floor on our knees while singing chants about how it takes blood, sweat, and tears to be a delta. Afterwards, many of us had bloody knees by the time we left.

There were other chants that required us to proclaim that we would "live and die" for Delta. There was an overwhelming amount of physical, verbal, mental, emotional, and spiritual abuse during these long nights. They made us work out, recite information, sing, cry, and so much more. Set is where all the damage was done to our mindsets that made us believe this was supposed to be our portion.

They told us that this part of the pledging process was to break us down in order to build us back up. They told us that we were supposed to be stronger as a result of our endurance in such horrifying experiences. This process was meant to create a bonding experience with our line sisters that we wouldn't have with anyone else. The line was supposed to become one. And while all those things did happen, it left very traumatic and dark scars on my heart and mind subconsciously. I believe they instilled fear into us so deeply that it muzzled us. The fear they implanted made us lie to everyone about this process in the name of discretion. It kept us from speaking up about how wrong it was.

Personally, I was extremely terrified and didn't know what to do or who to talk to. I used to go to set every night and pray to God that these women didn't bother me for the night. Unfortunately, my name was being called out of line every night for something. They labeled me as the girl from Detroit with a bad attitude. I felt like the prophytes hated me. They expressed it very well emotionally, verbally and physically. One night, they kidnapped me and a few others. I was taken to a house and made to sit in "delta chair" (a squat position with your arms held out and your head tilted back) while holding books in each arm.

Then they put us in a bathtub and flung mustard, relish and other condiments in our face and hair with a spoon while we recited information. After that, they made me sit in "delta chair" while they poured ice-cold buckets of water on my head and simultaneously held an activated taser next to my nose so that I wouldn't move from the position. My crying and screaming did nothing for them to stop. It was so bad that the girls with me even cried out for them to leave me alone. They then took us to a forest where our other line sisters had to come and find us. You would think the torture would've been over, but they made us crush eggs in each other's hair from the front of the line to the back once we were found.

That was the one night I was ready to give up. I cried for hours when we left. I believe I skipped all of my classes that day to stay in bed and cry. So many of my then line sisters showed me love, and encouraged me to stay. We were almost at the finish line when this happened, so it wouldn't have made sense to give up now. The crazy thing is this perseverance brainwashing didn't even come from them. During "set" we were made to recite the poem *See It Through* every time they felt like we were giving up. So for the sisters who encouraged me to stay, I completely understood why they did so.

I now realize how wicked the pledging process was. While I was in it, I was just trying to stick it out because of everything I had been told I would receive as a result of crossing this line. I wanted sisterhood. I wanted to serve my community with that sisterhood. I wanted to be a part of a prestigious group of black women known for academic excellence. I wanted the networks it came with. I wanted to wear the letters. I wanted to stroll and step on campus for everyone to see. I wanted the "it girl" status. I wanted to be known as the girl who didn't give up on something she put her mind to, no matter how hard it was. I was willing to submit my whole identity to the sorority as if God had not already given me an identity of my own.

I ignored every red flag that came with this organization, and I completed the pledging process. I passed the delta achievement test, went through the final initiation ritual, had a pinning ceremony and performed in a delta probate show (formal presentation to reveal new line members) on campus to seal the deal. Crossing into BLGOs is a highly esteemed badge of honor amongst collegiate professionals. It is actually praised at Historically Black College Universities (HBCUs) like the one I attended. That "achievement" was supposed to be the highlight of the spring for us. However, things took a turn for the worst.

That following week, we attended our very first delta meeting, and upon entrance, we were made to put all of our doctrine binders in a corner while each of us was taken to a private room to be interrogated for suspicious activity. We were then placed on Cease and Desist to undergo a serious investigation.

During the investigation, we found out that someone had gotten to headquarters about our intake process. Delta is supposed to be a non-hazing organization, which was told to us at Rush. However, the prophytes who brought in this line did not comply with the rules. Since hazing is illegal, they made us lie to the investigators about our process. In order to stay out of trouble, I lied. I'm pretty sure others lied as well, but that didn't matter. They suspended our chapter for 3 years. Although they had no evidence of hazing, they pinned our suspension on our probate show uniforms and called what we wore a disgrace to Delta.

The suspension was heartbreaking. I felt like I had just gone through hell and hot water to obtain these *greek letters* that I couldn't even wear on campus. All of the desires I had to stroll, step and flaunt my membership around were null and void. We continued to do these things amongst ourselves, at parties, and greek picnics. However, it wasn't the same as being able to show out on campus. I eventually got a campus apartment with some of my former line-sisters where we threw parties and had the best private delta life that we could have. We were lit. Our bond remained tight because it was all we had after that. We experienced so much together just to have it all ripped away from us. They were my main reason for holding on to Delta.

2

HOW IT ENDED

It Is That Deep

Over the 6 years that I spent in Delta, I did receive an amazing sisterhood. My former line sisters were a blessing to me. One of them gave me a job during my last year of college that helped me tremendously. We celebrated many accomplishments and life milestones together. When I graduated, I attended a prayer meeting with a regional chapter where I had a conversation with a former soror who encouraged me in my move to LA. When I moved to LA shortly after, I got my first job working with the BET Awards from a former soror. I met former sorors everywhere I went who were always nice, welcoming and willing to help me with whatever I needed. Everything promised to me about sisterhood, scholarship, service, and networking opportunities, I received.

I was an inactive member of the organization for 5 years. I never paid dues to be active because all of the benefits I hoped for were already at my fingertips. However, I wasn't where I wanted to be in my life. I remember seeing a video on YouTube of someone denouncing AKA sorority. I watched the entire thing in disbelief that they were doing rituals to be initiated that went against God. Once that video was over, I told myself that it had nothing to do with me. In my eyes, delta wasn't like that, and we didn't do the idolatrous things they did. I totally forgot about every ritual, chant, pledge, oath and hymn sung to Delta while being inactive. A few years later, God opened my eyes and brought to my remembrance that everything she said in that video resonated with me as well.

I had just moved into a one-bedroom apartment in North Hollywood, CA, when the world shut down in March of 2020. This was my very first time living alone, and here we were in a pandemic that would not allow me to go anywhere or have any company. This time was hard for me to adjust to because I was what I would consider a social butterfly before this happened. Eventually, I stopped crying about not being able to have human interactions, and I started spending more time with

God. This time with God led me to fasting and praying.

I decided to go on a 21-Day fast where I ate no food and drank water and apple juice the whole time. I was being pruned and undergoing a lot of self-deliverance. I was crying out to God everyday on this fast. I was purging, healing, being stripped of ideologies, changing, praying in the spirit a lot, and seeking God like never before. I was studying the Bible more and deeper than I used to. I was doing whatever I thought would bring me closer to God because I just knew it was my time to go higher in God. However, I noticed I was hitting a glass ceiling in certain areas of my spirit.

The fast concluded in early May of that year. After a fast, you would think everything was supposed to go smoothly, and all of my prayers were supposed to be answered. It did not work quite like that. I actually entered a period of intense spiritual warfare. My dream life was activated after that fast. I started having dreams galore. Most of the dreams were horrifying. It was like the whole kingdom of darkness was after me during that time. I was being chased, attacked, terrorized, and so much more in my dreams.

Having dreams like that led me on a YouTube search. I tried searching Google first. I learned quickly that googling dreams can be very dangerous and deceptive. Most of the dream interpretation sites on Google are witchcraft sites that lure people into agreement with things God doesn't have for them. After being deceived by Google's interpretations, I had to throw the Google searching dreams idea out the window. So I went to YouTube to search for someone who was a man or woman of God that was talking about dreams. That is when I found Minister Kevin Ewing.

His teachings were diving deep into dreams, biblical interpretations, spiritual warfare, fasting and praying, giving to the poor, illegal covenants, evil altars, and so many other spiritual things that I had no clue about before finding him. I felt like I had hit the spiritual knowledge jackpot on his channel. What I learned was that I had illegal covenants in the spirit realm that gave access to dark powers in order for them to attack me spiritually. I later found out that Delta was one of those covenants.

A covenant is a binding agreement between two parties. These covenants can be solidified by vows, promises, oaths, pledges, contracts, etc. Covenants are both natural and spiritual. An example of a natural covenant is the covenant of marriage. An example of a spiritual covenant is the covenant God made with Abraham when He promised to bless him in Genesis 12 verses 1 through 3. A spiritual covenant is a covenant you can not see. It is verbal. It is more binding than the physical covenant because spiritual forces are involved. Spiritual covenants are so deep that they can also be made or reinstated via dreams. This is what I was dealing with.

I remember watching one of Minister Ewing's videos "Discovering Hidden Covenants," where he taught about covenants made with unclean spirits, idols, and deities. These are the covenants that are illegal for children of God to come into agreement with. These illegal covenants open up the doors for the enemy to wreak havoc in a person's life and family. It is where generational curses stem from. He explained that the minute you agree to a covenant with an unclean spirit, then you are now under their god and not yours. The reason is that you can not serve two masters.

He began to give examples of how you can form these illegal covenants, and one of the examples was through secret societies. He specifically mentioned freemasonry and eastern star fraternal organizations when he spoke of this example. At that time, I didn't think Delta fell in the same category with those secret societies. So I didn't think that part of his teaching applied to me.

After taking all of my notes and grasping a full understanding of covenants, I ended the video feeling enlightened. However, I didn't think I had the exact answers to why I was struggling in my dreams, and why I felt like I was hitting a glass ceiling in my life spiritually. I decided to go through the comment section of that video when it was over. Since the video was about 3 years old at that time, many testimonies and agreements were shared that inspired me. Then I landed on a comment that asked the question, "Are you talking about Black Greek Letter Organizations too?" To my surprise, this was the one comment I saw a response from Minister Ewing, and he replied, "Yes, them too."

I was completely blown away. I almost wanted to respond and say, "I know you're lying!" But something about his answer struck me. I started to feel a conviction about the sorority I had never felt before. I began to do my research. In doing my research, I found an article online about how Christians can't serve the goddess of wisdom that Delta serves while simultaneously serving Jesus Christ. I was so confused because I didn't think I was serving another god. I knew that the official emblem for Delta is Minvera, the goddess of wisdom, but I thought it was just a regular organizational symbol. I was so spiritually immature when I pledged that I didn't know she was an idol. The article also explained how Christians should not take any oaths or pledges to idols.

That was enough for me to repent. I began praying and crying out to God that night. I repented for the oath I declared and pledges I made. I asked God to forgive me if I had done or said anything wrong pertaining to the organization. The ritual book and doctrine binder full of intake information that I owned was stored away in my cousin's garage at the time. So I didn't know exactly what declarations I was repenting for because I didn't remember them anymore. I felt like my heart of repentance was enough. So much so that I decided to keep all of the paraphernalia I had.

I told myself I didn't have to throw any of my delta things away because I repented already. I still wanted to wear my line jacket and DST hoodies. I still had journals with the Delta crest on them that I was using at the time. The red and white DST keychain on my keys was so cute that I couldn't possibly take it off.

I believe I kept all of the delta stuff I had because I wanted my repentance to remain a secret. I was still willing to wear the paraphernalia and hang out with the sorors, all while acting like nothing had changed.

Repenting for the pledge I made was to be solely between me and God. I stopped researching Delta after reading that one article because it was enough for me. I was ready to move on without dwelling on it or discussing it with anyone. During this time, I had a dream in which I was telling my line sisters that I had to denounce Delta. I brushed it aside, thinking that I had already done so.

The crazy dreams and nightmares persisted and, at one point, intensified. I remember being afraid to go to sleep for a while. I would stay up all night, waiting for the sun to rise before I could allow myself to rest. I'd sleep only about 2 to 3 hours before waking up for work. I was sleep-deprived and tired of it all. Simultaneously, the racial injustice upheaval during that time added to my weariness. All of this led me to embark on another fast, this time a 40-day liquid fast instead of 21.

During this fast, I went on a journey of learning spiritual warfare. I was gathering up my scriptures to fight with because God taught me via my dreams that praying the scriptures works. I started winning battles that were taking place in my dreams with the word of God. And as I grew spiritually, I began to hear God more clearly than before. I remember looking at a delta journal I had with the crest on it and feeling irritated in my spirit. I ripped the cover of the journal off and threw it away. I didn't even know why I did that. What I do know is it sparked my interest in doing the research again.

One day shortly after, I was watching a live YouTube broadcast with Minister Ewing and a woman named Dr. Alexis. He was telling her and her audience everything he had been teaching about in his videos. He touched on the topics of praying and fasting. He spoke about spiritual warfare. Then he went into evil covenants we as believers may have in our lives that could be infiltrating us and we don't even know it.

I began to reflect on my life and how a lot of areas in my life felt stagnant. I honestly wasn't happy with my life. I felt like I should've been further along in life. I felt like my dreams and passions for the things I wanted to do in life were placed on hold. It was like little doors would open for me here and there, but there was nothing to show for it. My life reflected the life of someone who was always "almost there, but not quite yet."

Minister Ewing explained how we can get ourselves into these evil covenants. When he mentioned secret societies, this time he included the topic of fraternities and sororities. The live chat went up after that. The comments were surprisingly filled with deltas who didn't agree, and also testimonies of ex-deltas who did agree. There were also people who had been descendants of

Freemasons sharing their testimonies. Other fraternity and sorority participants and family members of participants also shared their viewpoints.

Dr. Alexis went on to say that anyone in the body of Christ who has pledged in any fraternity or sorority is in error and needs to pray because you have opened up yourself to a god who is not the one and only true and living God. That's when it clicked for me.

Minivera wasn't just some symbol that represented the sorority I was a part of! This was a whole idol from the Roman and Greek religions. There are people in the world who actually serve this deity called Minerva. If the situation were reversed, and Greek citizens used man-made images of Jesus as emblems for their secret societies, it would be considered blasphemy!

When I had that revelation, I remembered all the times we knelt at altars to say things during the intake process. There was always a small table and a "torch of wisdom" candle lit on it. I recalled the "duck ceremony," where we had to name ducks that represented us at an altar. I remembered the candle wax ritual where they poured hot candle wax on our shoulders, and then we had to peel it off after it dried and keep it as some symbol of skin-to-skin connection. I remembered the song we sang at our probate that said, "all of my love, peace and happiness, I'm going to give to delta." All the memories of the things I said and did came rushing to my mind.

I realized that I never broke the covenant. I never renounced the things I thought I repented for. I never came out of agreement with delta sigma theta for real. I had only repented for what I thought could possibly be the issue, but I had no real revelation of what I was doing. At that moment, I was overwhelmed. I started crying and praying.

Then I picked up my phone and called one of my former line sisters, sobbing, and said, "WE GOTTA GET OUT OF DELTA!" I tried to explain why, and she told me that someone prophetic at her church had already shared this with her. They had told her to renounce the sorority in prayer. I asked her why she hadn't told me, and she admitted she didn't fully understand it at the time. So, I explained that Delta was an illegal covenant in the spiritual realm, and we had to break free from it. She agreed, and I began to pray for both of us.

I prayed for a very long time. I was crying out, repenting for us, renouncing everything I could remember saying, and pleading the Blood of Jesus. By the time I got off that phone, I knew some things had broken off of us in prayer. Since I was still in my 40-Day fast, I spent the rest of that time repenting, renouncing and coming out of agreement with everything concerning delta. I threw away all of the items and paraphernalia I had. I got rid of that key chain I wanted to keep before. I got rid of blankets, jackets, shirts, elephants and so much more. Then I remembered I needed to go to my cousin's house, who lived a few states away, to clear out his garage of all the stuff I had there from college. I eventually did and got rid of everything.

When the fast had ended, I was two weeks away from publishing my first book, *All Things Work Together*. I remember I talked a little about the delta life that I enjoyed in college in that book. When I got my book back from the editor, I had to change the line that said I was a member. I emphasized in that specific chapter that I was no longer a member of the organization. Then I announced the book on all my social media platforms.

Someone from college called and asked me if I could do a book signing at my college for the students. Then he mentioned he was a new advisor for the National Pan-Hellenic Council team that governed the BGLO's on campus. I knew he was insinuating that being an alumni and a delta would make the booking process easy and run smoothly. I told him that if I came, it would be as Porchia Carter and not "Porchia, the delta." He asked if any members from my chapter knew about my renouncement. I said no. He suggested I at least tell my line sisters, and I agreed.

That same day, I started telling my former line sisters in groups. I sent voice notes to a couple of group chats I was in with them. One of the group chats called me on a Group FaceTime to discuss what I was telling them. During that call, I felt like I was fighting for my faith. I told them that I got myself into illegal covenants in the spirit realm, and delta was one of those covenants. I now know that it was hard to understand without any background knowledge of what covenants are and how they operate in your life. We will discuss more of this in the next chapter.

After that call, I felt discouraged and didn't want to tell anyone else about my newfound freedom. Since I had never seen anyone denounce Delta publicly before, I went to YouTube to search for it. I entered "Denouncing Delta Sigma Theta," and that's where I found my now friend, Jasmine. Her video was the first one I felt drawn to watch. I deeply resonated with everything she explained. I gained new insight into why God had called me out of the organization and learned that renouncing wasn't enough; I needed to formally withdraw my membership from the sorority.

I reached out to her from the contact information listed in her description. I had so many questions for her that I sent via email, and she responded with a video. From then, she went on to assist with my formal denouncing process, which actually took us through a six month legal battle to complete. I will explain in the next chapter why that happened. Nevertheless, Jasmine and I are now great friends, and I am so glad God sent me someone to walk with in this journey. There's nothing like knowing you're not alone in a situation that you may feel nobody understands except you.

The terrible nightmare dreams I was having stopped after renouncing delta. That is how I knew my spirit was free. I knew that the demons that were attacking me in that particular area of my life no longer had access to me. I felt like a weight was lifted off of me. I felt like my prayers were no longer hitting a glass ceiling.

Shortly after renouncing, I had a dream that made me believe I had done the right thing. Before I share the dream, do you remember the sister I called and prayed with the night I decided to renounce? Let's call her Ana.

In this dream, I was with my former line sisters. We were all lined up to go somewhere. Everybody had on all black. We were about to do something illegal, and I knew it. I stepped out of line because I could no longer be a part. A few of them got really upset with me. I didn't care. I sat down. Then Ana came and sat down on my lap.

Everyone that remained in line started going off on me about my decision. One of them yelled at Ana and I to get back in line. Ana got up and got back in line with them. Instead of me doing the same, I left.

While I was leaving, a man started chasing me. I knew it was them who sent him after me. He was furious and trying to get me to kill me. I was running towards the office of the delta advisor who wrote my entry letter into the organization.

The guy that was chasing me got into an old-school-looking car. I outran the car and made it to the office. When I got inside, I saw a vision of what was happening outside. That car that the man was using to chase me blew up! The explosion destroyed him too.

After the car blew up, I thought everything was going back to normal. But I knew the girls were still trying to kill me. So, I pleaded with the advisor that we needed to leave. I handed her her keys from her drawer and told her to open the door so I could go. She opened it.

Before running out of there, I looked under her desk and saw another set of keys. I knew these keys belonged to me. I grabbed them and headed out of the door. And I believe I closed it behind me before waking up.

This was the dream where I knew I had done what was right. The part where Ana got back in line even came true. I saw Ana in the physical still participating in delta activities, although I thought we had renounced together. I didn't judge her. I still love her deeply and continue showing love to her to this very day. I believe that my dream prepared me for what was to come, and I thank God for being a revealer of all things.

I used to think and say the words, "it's not that deep," when I first began to contemplate renouncing and denouncing delta. I have since realized that if it was deep enough to affect my dream life, then there had to be more to the story than what I was aware of. I regret not doing any research about the origin of fraternities and sororities before getting involved. What I know now is that they are all the same. The spiritual implications that come with pledging are deep enough to negatively affect one's life. The benefits you are supposed to receive after pledging can only take you so far. However, it can not compete with the things God can do for you. No organization is or will ever be worth jeopardizing my relationship with God.

3

HOW TO GET FREE

Breaking Evil Covenants

Pledging into secret societies is indeed forming illegal covenants in the spirit realm. We must take this seriously because we are spiritual beings living a natural experience in life. There is nothing that happens naturally that doesn't first happen spiritually. If you are spiritually connected to what is not of God, how can He protect you from what those spiritual forces have access to perform in your life? It can only be by the mercies of God that you don't forfeit the promises that God has for you.

If you are tied to fraternities and sororities, and think nothing is wrong with it, please do your research! You may think your life is all good and you have no complaints, however the Bible is clear that God will visit the iniquities of His people for generations to come. (See Exodus 20:5; Deuteronomy 5:9; Numbers 14:18) If you don't break these illegal covenants for you, do it for your children and the generations that will come after you! They will suffer from all kinds of affliction in life due to what you did.

Understanding Covenants

In a literal sense, a covenant means a binding agreement, a legal contract. It is a seal of agreement between two or more parties.

- ⁑ Covenants can be both natural and spiritual covenants.

- ⁑ Natural covenants are visible, like the covenant of marriage.

- ⁑ Spiritual covenants are verbal, like the covenant God made with Abraham in Genesis 17:1-2 where He promised to multiply him exceedingly.

- ⁑ Spiritual covenants are more binding than physical covenants because spiritual forces are involved.

- ❖ All covenants come with conditions.

- ❖ Spiritual covenants can only be formed through human agreement. The reason being is that God gave humans dominion and authority over the earth in Genesis 1:28. This is like when we come into agreement with the Word of God for it to work for us.

- ❖ When a human comes into agreement with a spirit, whether good or bad, whatever the spirit represents can perform its will on the earth from that covenant.

- ❖ If someone breaches a covenant (does anything outside of the conditions of the covenant), consequences and whatever curses they have come with it. We see an example of this in the Bible when David experienced famine in the land during his reign as king in 2 Samuel 21:1-9. He experienced that famine because Saul, the king that preceded him, breached the covenant made between Joshua and the Gibeonites back in Joshua 9:1-21. Saul killed the Gibeonites. Although the covenant was made hundreds of years before Saul was born, the consequences of that covenant lasted for generations after the people who made it. David eventually rectified the situation through the help of God.

- ⚜ Unclean spirits actively seek human agreement to establish covenants, allowing them to infiltrate family bloodlines.

- ⚜ When covenants are breached, their consequences can last for generations in those bloodlines.

Secret Societies as Evil Covenants

Now, let's establish that secret societies, including fraternities and sororities, are covenants made with unclean spirits. Unclean spirits are spiritually impure, wicked, demonic, and not of God. There are several ways secret societies can be called out on being unclean; however, let's focus on the fact that every initiation into these organizations must go through a ritual.

> **Ritual**: the prescribed order of performing a ceremony, especially one characteristic of a particular religion or church.

If a ritual is a ceremony of a particular religion or church, what religion are we honoring when we perform these ceremonies for these Greek organizations? When you participate in rituals of any other religion, you are lifting up their god, and our God is not in that ceremony with you. For example, in the case of delta, during the initiation ritual, there is no clarity that the ritual is being performed for our Lord and Savior Jesus Christ. Instead, they light the "torch of wisdom" on an altar and recite the sorority motto. They claim that the "torch of wisdom burns whenever delta women are assembled, and guides their footsteps as they work in the name of the sorority." This has nothing to do with Jesus Christ, who is the true guide of our footsteps (see Psalm 32:8).

Also, in response to this declaration, the Bible tells us in Colossians 2:23-24 NKJV, "And whatever you do, do it heartily, as to the Lord and not to men, knowing that from the Lord you will receive the reward of the inheritance; for you serve the Lord Christ." Why would I then go do work in the name of a sorority? Is that not rebellion to what The Lord has spoken in His word?

There is also a line in the ritual that clearly states, "We believe in a spiritual life, but we leave to the individual the selection of the medium for its outward manifestation." They are giving people options of what god they want to serve during this ritual. They lack clarity in the "Christian principles" they claim to be founded on. All the other BGLO's are the same.

Find any ritual from these organizations and thoroughly read the actions, declarations and decrees of the rituals. Compare line by line what they say versus the Word of God. Delta's initiation ritual is public knowledge, and can be found with a quick Google search. I have also found a few of the others via Google. If you are serious about serving God and God alone, seek Him on whether these rituals are of Him or not. Once you do your due diligence in research, you will find that the origins and foundation of all of these secret societies are not of God and are considered unclean in the realms of the spirit.

> *"Therefore "Come out from among them and be separate, says the Lord. Do not touch what is unclean, And I will receive you.""* - 2 Corinthians 6:17 NKJV

Furthermore, these rituals are usually performed at altars. Altars are the place where divinity and humanity meet in order to form covenants. You must ask yourself what deity is at the meeting place of these altars during the rituals performed? In the next section of this chapter we will discover what deities are present for these rituals in BLGOs.

The covenants with fraternities and sororities must be broken to deepen your relationship with God. If you think you've reached a good place with God and need not go further, you're mistaken. There is no "arrival" in our relationship with God; we are meant to go from glory to glory (2 Corinthians 3:18). Every area of our lives must reflect God's glory, and when we feel like we're hitting glass ceilings or experiencing stagnation, it's essential to examine our spiritual covenants.

How To Break Covenants With Secret Societies

Step 1: Understand Why What You Are A Part Of Is Wrong

> *"My people are destroyed for lack of knowledge. Because you have rejected knowledge, I also will reject you from being priest for Me; Because you have forgotten the law of your God, I also will forget your children."* - Hosea 4:6 NKJV

If you don't know why what you are doing is wrong, you won't have the conviction to leave when God is telling you to leave. When you see others coming out of these organizations, you will try to contend with them as if they are your enemy.

Pride will begin to consume you, which can lead to the danger of being resisted by God (*see James 4:6*). A lot of individuals in BLGOs take pride in their organization. I know because I took pride in delta. However, pride surely does come before destruction (*see Proverbs 16:18*).

Before my destruction, God saved me. He didn't let me go too far off on the deep end to where I became unreachable. I had times when I would see someone publicly denouncing a BGLO and would shrug my shoulders thinking, "well that's them." I thought it didn't apply to me because I never saw a delta denouncing. It wasn't until I was already called out that I began to see other women of God denouncing the sorority. What I have learned in this whole thing is that these organizations are all the same. They speak the same languages. They have the same clauses. They all worship deities. They were all founded on the basis of idolatry.

From the beginning of the pledge process to the final initiation and day-to-day operations, these organizations go against the word of God.

Anything that goes against God's word is from the kingdom of darkness. The enemies of your soul want to keep you in the dark about these organizations because they want to destroy you. They want you bound.

The covenant you make with these unclean spirits opens doors for them to cause affliction, delay, destruction and so many other negative things in any area of your life that they choose. I lacked knowledge of the spiritual implications of the choice I made to pledge. However, Jesus told us in John 8:32 that when we know the truth, that truth will make us free!

Here are some truths about how fraternities and sororities go against the word of God:

> "And Jesus answered and said to him, "Get behind Me, Satan! For it is written, 'You shall worship the Lord your God, and Him only you shall serve.'" - Luke 4:8 NKJV

When you join these organizations, you both worship and serve them knowingly or unknowingly. As we already discussed concerning rituals, once the rituals are performed, you have lifted up the god of that organization in participation in these religious ceremonies. Many of us went through the initiation rituals with the excitement of crossing the finish line rather than listening to everything being said. We pledged our agreement without a full understanding of how idolatrous these actions were. The declarations and spoken pledges go against what Jesus said in the abovementioned scripture. These organizations are idolatrous and serve other gods even though Jesus told us to serve The Lord and Him only.

During these ceremonies, each of these organizations sing hymns as a step in the rituals. They also sing hymns in chapter meetings and other special services. A **hymn** is a religious song or poem of praise to God or a god. If there is no other god associated with these organizations, why on earth would hymns be sung to the organization in reverence to it? This is considered worship. This also goes against what Jesus said to satan in the scripture above. For instance, Delta has a hymn that begins with the lyrics, "Delta! With glowing hearts we praise thee...". This hymn elevates the god of "Delta." Similar hymns are sung in other organizations, all of which are worshiping and exalting their respective gods. This should be considered unacceptable to true believers in Jesus Christ because hymns belong to the Lord.

One of the things members of these organizations always point out in an argument about "what's right" is that they do community service. They love to boast about serving and uplifting communities with their programs and initiatives to make a change. However, they do service to their communities in honor and in the name of their organizations, not The Lord. Some of them even require members to work "in the spirit of" their organization. As we mentioned in Colossians 2:23-24, your work is always supposed to be as unto our Lord Jesus Christ because that is who we serve. If community service is such an important aspect of one's life, they should be able to perform that service without the backing of a secret society.

Due to the covenants of secrecy, the organizations try to hide their roots and what they stem from. The origin of all fraternities and sororities can be traced back to the foundation of freemasonry. Freemasonry is occultic. These fraternities and sororities adopt certain characteristics from freemason ideals and goals. What's worse than that is each of these organizations have a deity associated with the creation of what they represent. I did a quick Google search for the BGLO's deity representations, and here is what I found:

> Alpha Phi Alpha Fraternity Inc: Sphinx of Giza - Egyptian god
>
> Omega Psi Phi Fraternity Inc: Anubis - Egyptian god
>
> Kappa Alpha Psi Fraternity Inc: Apollo - Greek god/Thoth - Egyptian god
>
> Phi Beta Sigma Fraternity Inc: Horus - Egyptian god
>
> Iota Phi Theta Fraternity Inc: Centaur - Egyptian god

Alpha Kappa Alpha Sorority Inc: Qetesh - Semitic goddess

Delta Sigma Theta Sorority Inc: Minerva - Roman goddess

Zeta Phi Beta Sorority Inc: Bastet - Egyptian goddess

Sigma Gamma Rho Sorority Inc: Aurora - Roman goddess

All of the gods and goddesses of these organizations come from different religions. Greek, Roman and Egyptian people actually worship these gods regardless of how other people around the world use them as "emblems". That means they are idols! An idol is an image or representation of a god used as an object of worship. These idols are the deities that are present during the rituals performed in these organizations.

If you are members of these organizations, you have come into agreement with them, and are now operating in idolatry. Whether you feel like you idolize your organization or not, if the foundation of that organization is idolatry, then you come into agreement with it when you pledge your loyalty to it. That is how the illegal covenant is formed. God is clear about how He feels about idolatry! (see Exodus 20:3-6)

> "Who may ascend into the hill of the Lord? Or who may stand in His holy place? He who has clean hands and a pure heart, Who has not lifted up his soul to an idol, Nor sworn deceitfully." - Psalms 24:3-4 NKJV

This scripture above is how we can truly ascend in the presence of God as believers. However, these secret societies have deceived God's people into idolatry, placing a barrier to ascension with The Lord. The deceit is so great that members of these organizations argue that because their Ministers, Pastors, Bishops, etc., are also members, it must be acceptable to God. That is far from the truth. When God said, "My People" perish for lack of knowledge, that is what He meant. Just because you are "God's People" and believe you have gotten away with idolatry for the time being doesn't mean it is right. God is a merciful God, and it is only by His mercies that the consequences of our decisions do not consume us.

The issue is that idolatry opens doors for the kingdom of darkness to afflict the people of God. Most people in the body of Christ who are also in these organizations may be dealing with things they can't share. They may also be having issues in areas of their life that are supposed to have ease in them. They may even be dealing with stagnancy, delay, and little to no progress in their endeavors. Their lives may look completely opposite to what they have been praying to see. Deception makes you sign the dotted line to a contract that is not good for you. One that will eventually rob you of things that belong to you. That is how these secret societies operate. You never know what area of your life or generation you have given the enemy legal and free range to manipulate when you make that pledge.

These organizations also swear deceitfully when they do decide to add scripture references to their rituals. They paraphrase or manipulate the scriptures to fit the organization's purpose for that moment. I remember when I went back to my cousin's garage to find all of my old delta things to get rid of; I went through the doctrine I had. What I found made my stomach turn. There is something in the ritual book called the "delta meditation." In this meditation, delta takes the Bible passage 1 Corinthians 13 and replaces the word "love" with the "Delta" and "soror". In verse 11 of 1 Corinthians 13, they replace the word "child" with "pyramid," which is what you are called while on line. And they replace the word "man" with "Delta". This is unacceptable and should be seen as unacceptable to true believers of Jesus Christ.

> *"Lying lips are an abomination to the Lord, but those who deal truthfully are His delight."* - **Proverbs 12:22**

These organizations teach you to lie! You are supposed to keep their secrets through lies. You are supposed to cover up their wrongdoings with lies. I lied about everything while I was on line because they told us to. I had to lie to my friends who didn't know I was pledging. I had to lie to the delta advisor who kept asking me if we were meeting up at night. I had to lie to my professors about why I was so tired in class. I even lied to my family members who asked me if I was being hazed. I lied to the investigators who came to question us about our intake process when the chapter was under investigation.

Throughout the process of pledging that sorority, and even after crossing into it, there was not a truthful bone in my body concerning the organization. All we did was lie. That's what we were taught. The moment they told us to turn our locations off on our phones that very first night, I should have known I would spend the rest of that process lying to cover up my whereabouts.

An abomination is a thing that causes disgust or hatred. According to the scripture above, that is what I became to God. That is what all of His people become when we lie for these secret societies. The worst part is we no longer are children of God after telling lies. Jesus told us in John 8:44 that we become children of the devil because he is the father of lies. Lying was my most extended area of repentance because I know now how much God hates it.

> *"The violence of the wicked will destroy them, Because they refuse to do justice."* **Proverbs 21:7 NKJV**

These fraternities and sororities abuse and manipulate people with their violence. They beat you for entrance into their organizations. They beat you into fear of telling the truth about what they did to you. They bring harm to the bodies of people pledging in various ways. They have even brought people to the point of death with their wickedness of abuse. This is not of God! God hates it. His word says in Psalms 11:5 NKJV *"The Lord tests the righteous, But the wicked and the one who loves violence His soul hates."* Desiring to have power and authority over people entering an organization is not worth being hated by God.

Our bodies are temples of the Holy Ghost. He does not condone the beating, bruising, or branding of His temple. His temple doesn't have to be broken down and built back up. He is God, and His temple is perfect the way He made it. Jesus was already beaten and bruised for our sins before we were born.

He paid the price in His body for us to be redeemed, atoned, and made children of God. We should not be paying the same manner of price that He paid in order for us to join organizations that are not of Him from the start.

For the people who pledged into these secret societies without having to go through an underground process or any form of hazing, you still should not be a part of them. You most likely had more time on your hands to really do your research. You could have thoroughly gone through every ritual, oath, hymn, chant, and underlying facts of these organizations without any interference. The pledging period should have been easier for you to gain a true understanding of what you were signing up for. Just because you did not participate in the physical abuse aspect of pledging to the organization does not mean you are exempt from being held accountable for the idolatry that comes with being a member.

> *"Then Jesus spoke to them again, saying, "I am the light of the world. He who follows Me shall not walk in darkness, but have the light of life." -* John 8:12 NKJV

These fraternities and sororities all claim to be light. They say things like "see the light of "whatever Greek letter they represent." Delta in particular, has a song that says, "I see the light, I see the delta light, shining down on me..." How does a Greek letter organization have light that shines down on someone? This doesn't make sense. When they claim they are light, they are in representation of Satan. In 2 Corinthians 11:14, the Bible says, "And no wonder! For Satan himself transforms himself into an angel of light." This is the only explanation for these organizations calling themselves light.

> *"And you shall love the Lord your God with all your heart, with all your soul, with all your mind, and with all your strength.' This is the first commandment. And the second, like it, is this: 'You shall love your neighbor as yourself.' There is no other commandment greater than these." - Mark 12:30-31 NKJV*

A few of these fraternities and sororities have songs that express they give "All of their love, heart, mind, soul and strength" to their organization. Both delta and omega members sing the "All of My Love" songs during their probates. They also serenade members of the organization for lifetime achievements and accomplishments. During the serenading, they sing songs unto their organization. For instance, delta serenades its members with their "sweetheart song." This song basically states that no matter who a delta woman may love, if she wears a delta symbol, then her first love is "DST." This is both disrespectful to God and the newlywed husband when sung to women on their wedding days. God tells us in Revelation 2:4-5 that He is our first love, and when we leave our first love, He will remove our lampstand.

For the second commandment stated by Jesus in this text, to love your neighbor as yourself is to do good to them. The way some of the members of these organizations treat people shows that they either don't love people or don't love themselves. They treat people horribly just to be part of the organizations. They take people's money. They fight with people who pledge to a different organization than them. They become campus bullies to people they don't like. They "run the yard" and behave rudely to people who are not "greek." They don't show love the way God tells us to.

When you become a member of these organizations, they will show love as long as you are always in agreement with what they believe. The minute someone decides to renounce and denounce their organization, "loving your neighbor" goes out the window for them. They show them the opposite of love. They exile them, talk bad about them, and then they treat them like they never existed.

> "For all that is in the world—the lust of the flesh, the lust of the eyes, and the pride of life—is not of the Father but is of the world." - I John 2:16 NKJV

We are going to tackle a few things in this one scripture. These fraternities and sororities are worldly. How they maneuver, and the things they do on most college campuses are of this world and not of God. These organizations are, first and foremost, prideful! They boast about being "Greek," even though most of these members are of African descent. They boast about these greek letters they earned through beatings and other ungodly sacrifices. They boast in the chants they scream out during stepping, strolling and participating in campus gatherings. The fraternity members boast about being able to get whatever girl they want with their Greek status, while the sorority women boast about grasping the attention of men.

They also make people feel beneath them. Most of these organizations have built-in plots on the yard of the campus. Plots are constructed to symbolically and physically represent each organization's presence on campus. When people who aren't in these organizations sit or stand in their plots, they disrespectfully make them leave. They become yard bullies to protect monuments that they shouldn't have as Christians, according to Leviticus 26:1. They take pride in these organizations to the point of wanting to physically fight for them if they believe non-Greek members aren't respecting them.

Most of these organizations also promote lust. They advocate for sexual immorality on college campuses in subliminal ways. Some of these male organizations have underground pledge processes where the whole new line has to sleep with one girl in order to cross into the organization. Some of these organizations make it seem okay to have multiple sexual partners just because of their "Greek status." They operate in and promote perversion.

They throw parties that promote drunkenness. Each of these organizations has their own alcoholic beverage named after their organization. They encourage people to drink their juices, punch, and "oils" in order to have a good time at their gatherings. Most of these organizations express what it looks like to have the lust of the flesh, the lust of the eyes and the pride of life controlling their actions.

> *"This Book of the Law shall not depart from your mouth, but you shall meditate in it day and night, that you may observe to do according to all that is written in it. For then you will make your way prosperous, and then you will have good success."* - Joshua 1:8 NKJV

This debunks the networking excuse of being a part of these organizations. People believe that if they become a member of these groups, they will have prosperity and success in life due to the connections made in these secret societies. However, God says meditating on His word day and night should be our focus. If we meditate on His word, and actually live out His word, that is what guarantees our prosperity and good success. Whenever you depend on what people can do for you more than what God can do for you, then you are in trouble! God doesn't want any person or secret society to get the glory for what He does in your life. All glory belongs to Him and Him alone.

God also said in Psalm 1:1-3 NKJV

> *"⁽¹⁾ Blessed is the man Who walks not in the counsel of the ungodly, Nor stands in the path of sinners, Nor sits in the seat of the scornful; ⁽²⁾ But his delight is in the law of the Lord, And in His law he meditates day and night. ⁽³⁾ He shall be like a tree Planted by the rivers of water, That brings forth its fruit in its season, Whose leaf also shall not wither; And whatever he does shall prosper."*

The counsel of the ungodly are these organizations because they are ungodly. Standing in the path of sinners is participating in these organizations and most of their operations, picnics, conventions and gatherings. We all know how scornful members of these organizations can get in any situation of discord. So, if you are in these organizations, you are not like the tree planted by the rivers of water in verse 3, because you are dwelling in the opposite side of verse 1 of this passage. If you have made your way to verse 2 of this passage, where it says meditating on God's word day and night, then you would know what His word says against these organizations and you would stay free and clear of them. You would also walk in that truth regardless of what the scornful has to say. In order to prosper in all that we do, we must stay out of the forbidden mentions of verse 1, and dwell in verse 2 in order to experience verse 3 of this passage.

> *"God is Spirit, and those who worship Him must worship in spirit and truth."* - **John 8:24 NKJV**

All of these secret societies have a spirit behind them. They tell you that you are supposed to do things in these organizations with your mind, body and spirit. Unknowingly to them, they worship that spirit while pledging, participating in rituals, saying the ungodly chants and singing their idolatrous hymns. For instance, Alpha phi alpha fraternity has a prayer that starts off saying, "Oh Lord, may the true spirit of fraternity rule our hearts, guide our thoughts and control our lives..." What is the true spirit of fraternity? The scripture above tells us that God is Spirit. So if the Holy Spirit isn't who is ruling your heart, guiding your thoughts and controlling your life, what are you really being controlled by? The gods and goddesses that we went over a few scriptures before tell you what spirit is operating behind these "Greek letters" that they go so hard about.

Worship is more than just the slow songs we sing at church. Worship is our day-to-day living. Worship is what we give our time to. Worship is what we give our thoughts to. Worship is how we respond to God's word and whether or not we apply

His word to our daily lives. The scripture mentioned above is Jesus' words. He said this, not me. Anyone who believes in Jesus must also believe that He does not lie. He is the truth. His Spirit is the only true spirit we should be worshiping in spirit and in truth.

Step 2: Make A Decision

> *"And if it seems evil to you to serve the Lord, choose for yourselves this day whom you will serve, whether the gods which your fathers served that were on the other side of the River, or the gods of the Amorites, in whose land you dwell. But as for me and my house, we will serve the Lord.""* - Joshua 24:15 NKJV

You must decide who will be god or God in your life. The Bible tells us in Matthew 6:24 that we cannot serve two masters. If God is God, serve Him! If He is not God, serve your secret societies.

Step 3: Pray and Fast to Break Demonic Covenants

If you have chosen to serve God, who is our Lord and Savior, Jesus Christ, then you must break the illegal covenants with all secret societies and organizations that are not of Him! You do this in Prayer and Fasting. I want to be clear that you can pray for repentance and renunciation without being on a fast. However, I personally believe this is one of those things Jesus was talking about when He said, *"thing kind does not go out except by prayer and fasting"* in Matthew 17:21 NKJV.

Biblical fasting is to humble yourself by abstaining from all food for a period of time for the purpose of seeking The Lord. That period when you are not eating is spent reading God's Word, praying, worshiping, praising God, and intentionally focusing on Him. Fasting kills your flesh, enables your spiritual helpers, and realigns you to God's will.

I believe anyone who went through an underground process for these secret societies should know what it feels like to miss a meal or two because we ate very little during the pledging process. There were also food restrictions for delta, like not eating spaghetti or anything red that was close to the sorority's color. We sacrificed our bodies, sleep and eating for a period of time for these organizations, so surely we can turn our plates over for The Lord. Our flesh was sacrificed to get in these covenants, and our flesh needs to be sacrificed to get out. That is my opinion.

Here is what the Bible says concerning how you should fast:

> "'Is this not the fast that I have chosen: To loose the bonds of wickedness, To undo the heavy burdens, To let the oppressed go free, And that you break every yoke? Is it not to share your bread with the hungry, And that you bring to your house the poor who are cast out; When you see the naked, that you cover him, And not hide yourself from your own flesh? Then your light shall break forth like the morning, Your healing shall spring forth speedily, And your righteousness shall go before you; The glory of the Lord shall be your rear guard. Then you shall call, and the Lord will answer; You shall cry, and He will say, 'Here I am.' "If you take away the yoke from your midst, The pointing of the finger, and speaking wickedness, If you extend your soul to the hungry And satisfy the afflicted soul, Then your light shall dawn in the darkness, And your darkness shall be as the noonday. The Lord will guide you continually, And satisfy your soul in drought, And strengthen your bones; You shall be like a watered garden, And like a spring of water, whose waters do not fail. Those from among you Shall build the old waste places; You shall raise up the foundations of many generations; And you shall be called the Repairer of the Breach, The Restorer of Streets to Dwell In." - Isaiah 58:6-12 NKJV

This passage gives you a detailed description of what should be taking place both spiritually and naturally while you fast. There are many more scriptures in the Bible that talk about fasting, so if you need more please find whatever you need in God's word to help you. Lastly, Jesus said this should be between you and God in Matthew 6:16-18. Pray and ask God if He wants you to fast, how long, and what type of fast to do. He will guide you.

Also, pray and ask God to reveal to you the truth about these secret societies. Don't just take what you read or hear from anyone else. Get a revelation for yourself so that when the enemies try to come for you, which they will, you will have the truth God gave you to stand on. It's not enough to take a warning and run with it. This is your opportunity to be diligent in your walk with Christ by studying to show yourself approved. Study His word and compare it to the "secrets" of these organizations. You will indeed find that they are very deceptive and do not coincide with the word of God.

There are 3 things you need to do while praying and fasting...

Repent:

To repent means to turn away from sin and turn to God for forgiveness. This is where you confess everything you have said and done while being a member of these secret societies. Whether you remember everything or not, call it out and confess. Confess the sin of idolatry. In your confession, you must have a disgust for the things you committed that disgust God. This confession must come from the depths of your heart, mind and soul. He promises in 1 John 1:9 NKJV that "if we confess our sins, He is faithful and just to forgive us our sins and to cleanse us from all unrighteousness."

You must also be free and clear of all unforgiveness in your heart so that God may forgive you. Please see Matthew 6:14-15 for an explanation of why forgiveness is so important during repentance.

Renounce:

To renounce means to disown; to disclaim; to reject a title or claim; to refuse to own or acknowledge as belonging to (something); to sever any bond or claim that may exist (with something); to declare against something; to reject or decline formally.

You must renounce the oath you took. You must renounce the pledges you declared. You must renounce the chants you spoke. You must renounce all songs and hymns you sang to these secret societies. You must renounce your agreement with idolatry. You must renounce all lies, deceit, violence, lust, pride and vanity you may have taken part in with these organizations! You must come out of agreement with these fraternities and sororities as a whole.

Here are a few renunciations prayer points you can pray...

I would suggest starting off all prayers with the A.C.T.S. prayer method. It consists of

- **Adoration** (see 1 Chronicles 29:11-14 and Psalms 145 for examples)
- **Confession** (see Psalms 51:1-15)
- **Thanksgiving** (see Psalms 100:1-5)
- **Supplications** (see Philippians 4:6 and John 14:13)

Pray in that order of topics, then add the prayer points below...

- Lord, I renounce and revoke my membership with (name secret society) in the name of Jesus.

- I renounce all covenants I have made with (name the secret society) in the name of Jesus.

- I renounce all oaths, pledges and vows I made to the altars of secret societies (name them) in the name of Jesus.

- I reject and renounce all names given to me from these secret societies in the name of Jesus.

- I renounce and come out of agreement with all chants I spoke and songs I sang to (name secret society)

- I renounce, reject, and come out of agreement with anything negative spoken over my life in these organizations in the name of Jesus!

- I renounce all ungodly soul ties and immoral relationships formed as a result of these organizations in the name of Jesus.

- I renounce and come out of agreement with idolatry in the name of Jesus.

- I renounce all ungodly thought patterns and belief systems in the name of Jesus.

- I renounce, reject and revoke any known or unknown evil covenant that would try to keep me bound to (name the secret society) in the name of Jesus!

- Oh Lord, I come into agreement with the new covenant made by the death and resurrection of Jesus Christ to redeem me and give me the promise of eternal inheritance according to Hebrews 9:15 in the name of Jesus!

- Heavenly Father, I place you back on the throne of my heart where you belong, and I make you the sole ruler and Lord of my life in Jesus' name, Amen.

There are so many more prayer points you can pray to renounce and break these covenants; this is just to start you off.

Plead the Blood Of Jesus:

The blood of Jesus Christ is a powerful element of our faith. His blood is what was shed when He died for our sins and rose again from the grave. Hebrews 9:14 NKJV says, "how much more shall the blood of Christ, who through the eternal Spirit offered Himself without spot to God, cleanse your conscience from dead works to serve the living

God?" This means His blood thoroughly cleanses our hearts, minds, souls, and spirits from sinful impurities. It helps us to worship and serve God wholeheartedly.

The Bible also says we have victory in the blood of Jesus in Revelations 12:11. We are redeemed back to God by His blood in Ephesians 1:7. We are justified and made righteous by the blood of Jesus in Romans 5:9. One of the best things the Bible tells us about the blood of Jesus is that it speaks for us. Hebrews 12:24 NKJV says, "to Jesus the Mediator of the new covenant, and to the blood of sprinkling that speaks better things than that of Abel." This confirms that we are a part of the new covenant, and because of that covenant, His blood speaks better things for us. This is the blood that you need to plead over your life!

Plead the Blood Of Jesus Christ over everything concerning you. Plead the Blood of Jesus Christ over your mind, body, soul, heart, spirit, relationships, finances, businesses, ministries, careers, family, homes, cars, and everything else concerning you. Plead the Blood of Jesus against evil pronouncement trying to prevent your life from breaking the covenants. Your life must be covered in the Blood of Jesus. Everything connected to you must be covered under the Blood of Jesus. This will seal the new covenant in God and help you to move forward in victory!

Step 4: Formally Withdraw from the organization

Send a Letter to National Headquarters

To formally renounce and denounce delta, I had to send a Letter of Renouncement to the grand chapter of the organization. I found the contact information of the person overseeing the Department for Membership Policies and Procedures at the National Headquarters (NH). Then I had to find the contact information for the regional director/representative of the area I was living in. Once I drafted my letter, I emailed it to the NH membership representative and copied the regional director. I also sent copies of the letter so that they had a wet signature from me and physical documentation for their files. Please note that letters have to be notarized when sent via mail.

The regional director then contacted me for an exit interview a few weeks later. The interview was conducted with a regional representative. During this interview, she was basically trying to convince me to stay. She let me know that delta is a Christian-based organization, and we both serve the same god. I expressed that I had a different revelation due to illegal covenants delta places people in and that my

God has called me out of it. I confirmed to her that I was indeed withdrawing my membership. She informed me that she would send over the documents I needed to sign in order to complete my withdrawal request.

The documents I received via email from them were a Non-Disclosure Agreement (NDA) and a Renouncement Acknowledgement Form to sign. When reading through the documents, I realized they contained language that would keep me bound to the secrecy of the organization in order to withdraw. The NDA actually had a check box that read, "Covenant not to disclose" and I was required to check that box in order to sign the form. I did not sign that NDA.

I got my lawyer involved and requested that they remove my name from their system without having to sign their forms. I told them that I had just broken covenants with this organization, so I was not about to enter into a new covenant just to keep their secrets. This stance took me through a six month legal battle. I don't know all the back and forth that was happening between my lawyer and delta's lawyers, but I do know it got back to one of my former line sisters somehow.

That's when I knew I was shaking up the system. They eventually sent a brand-new Renouncement Acknowledgement and Confirmation Form that did not contain the NDA associated language. I later found out that this is the new form for their withdrawal process. After signing and returning, they sent me a Receipt of Completed Membership Withdrawal Form. This was the official letter that removed me from their system. This was the process for me, and I am sure the process is similar across the board.

- ❖ Find the Membership Renouncement and Withdrawal process and procedures of the organization you are leaving.

- ❖ Find the contact information of all individuals who need to be notified in this process.

- ❖ Write your letter telling them who you are and why you are withdrawing membership, and ask them for all necessary steps to confirm completion of the process. Then send it.

- ❖ Stand strong in your truth, and don't let anyone try to persuade you to stay in these organizations in the exit interviews.

- ❖ If the forms you are requested to sign are not in agreement with what God's word says, seek legal counsel if necessary.

- ❖ Get your Receipt of Completed Membership Withdrawal from these organizations!

Get Rid of All Items Connected to these Organizations

- ❖ Get rid of all gifts, books, clothing paraphernalia, jewelry, paddles, blankets, key chains, pens, badges, license plate frames, and decorations for your homes, cars, offices, and any places you may have decorated with these items.

- ❖ In the organization items and paraphernalia, evil spirits have a point of contact where they can legally travel in and out of your home and life. Please don't think you will be able to keep anything given to you or bought by you for these organizations. If you feel like you want to keep something, burn it! That is evidence there is an unclean spiritual attachment to that thing, and it must be destroyed.

Denounce

To denounce means to publicly declare (something) to be wrong or evil. It is my suggestion that you should notify the people you pledged with that you are no longer a part of the secret society. A few months after renouncing, I got my former line sisters together on a Zoom call to discuss that I had renounced the sorority. It was important for me to share this information with them because they saw me come into it with them, and I wanted no confusion about my position while leaving. I also love and care about them enough to share the truth with them. The majority of them understood and were in full support of my decision. I believe everyone you share this information with is completely up to you and should be Holy Spirit-led.

I also left all group chats and Facebook groups pertaining to the sorority. I had to eventually start notifying more people because I was still getting messages on fouder's day and anniversary celebrations of crossing. Then, two years after I renounced the organization, God prompted me to publicly denounce it on YouTube. Those prompts also happened in my dreams, like everything else pertaining to leaving the organization. The video went viral and also made me a YouTube partner. I did not expect the overwhelming responses of support I received, but I am grateful for having been obedient in sharing my denouncement story.

I remember a good friend of mine telling me one day, "you went into the organization publicly for the world to see, now you have to come out publicly." I was against that notion for a while. Then I had to ask myself what I was afraid of. Psalms 27:1 tells me how The Lord is my light and salvation, so whom shall I fear? And who shall I be afraid of?" I had to shake what I thought people would say or how people would receive me. (I will discuss more of this in the next chapter.) Also, dreams concerning delta hadn't happened in over a year before it was time to denounce it publicly, so I knew it was God.

I am not saying that everyone who renounces and denounces has to go public on social media platforms concerning it. However, I will leave you with Ephesians 5:11 NKJV, which says,

> *"And have no fellowship with the unfruitful works of darkness, but rather expose them."*

Step 5: Rejoice!

Rejoice that the covenant has been broken! Thank God for saving you! Thank God for saving your bloodline and your generation after you! Thank God for the curses you may have broken as a result of breaking the evil covenants! Rejoicing for what God has done for you shows Him gratitude! He could have left you in your darkness, but He gave you light instead.

Whenever you are thankful to God for anything, He always does more. Maybe you need God to reveal more things about your life that could be hindering the progress or prosperity of your destiny. Once He sees that you are receptive to knowledge, He will begin to share more with you. Rejoice in the higher heights and deeper depths you are about to encounter with God!!

> *"Rejoice in the Lord always. Again I will say, rejoice!"* - Philippians 4:4 NKJV

4

HOW TO NAVIGATE THE TRANSITION

Please God, Not People

God calling me out of delta was a transition I didn't know I needed. Stripping away the identity I had created for myself to embrace God's true identity for me was incredibly challenging. Life's transitions are never easy. When God calls us out of one situation and into another, it becomes our responsibility to navigate the discomfort of the unknown with unwavering faith, trusting in His plan.

When I renounced and only told those few groups of people I mentioned in chapter 2, I didn't want to talk about it anymore after that. Somehow the word started to travel slowly but surely without me knowing. I was preparing to attend a wedding for a former line sister a month after renouncing. I called Jasmine to help me navigate what I was supposed to do and how I was supposed to behave around my friends who were no longer my sorority sisters, although all of them didn't know it yet. She helped me as much as she could, but when I got there, all of her help went out the window.

Before traveling to the event, the bride texted me and requested that I wear a certain color. This was a tradition that all the line sisters wear a particular color in support of the bride at her wedding. I texted the bride that I would only wear the color she asked me to wear because she requested it. However, I am not wearing the color as a delta because I am no longer a delta. She never responded, so I took that as a mutual agreement for what I explained. (Lol).

When I got to the wedding, everything was beautiful, and I was able to connect with my former line sisters as if nothing had changed. After the ceremony, during cocktail hour, one of them pulled to the side to have a talk. Her talk turned out to be a confrontation. She asked me what I was doing there and why I was dressed like them since I claimed to no longer be a delta. She told me that I was causing confusion and that she had issues with my decisions. I clarified that I came because I was invited, and I wore the color in respect to the bride's request. I want to briefly try to explain my position and why I was no longer a delta, but the conversation was seemingly unprogressive. As I was walking away from the conversation that had ended in a very weird way, she said to me, "Whatever you do, just don't make YouTube video." I answered her, saying, "I don't plan on doing so, but if The Lord leads me to, I will."

Shortly after, the reception started, and right before my meal, another former line sister asked me why I haven't told everyone about my renouncement yet. She told me she found out through other people who weren't even a part of the sorority. The only person I told outside of the few group chats regarding this was the guy who called me from college. I then knew how things were going around. I believe I tried to explain to her that I didn't feel ready to tell everyone because people just don't understand. She ended the conversation telling me that I needed to own my truth.

At that moment, my appetite left me. Caught between the weighty conversation I'd had outside and the one now unfolding at the table, I felt overwhelmed. I barely ate anything; however, since it was an open bar reception, I went to get a glass of wine. I started drinking the wine to suppress the anxiety I was now feeling at the wedding. Before I knew it, I had about 3 refills. Then they started the "calling all deltas to the floor" song to prepare for the serenade. At that moment, my heart dropped.

I knew for sure I could not go circle up with them and sing that idolatrous sweetheart song. However, I didn't want anyone to notice that I wasn't going over there either. I decided to run to the bathroom. On my way there, someone who recognized me asked, "aren't you supposed to be going to the floor?" I shook my head no and just kept on walking. When I got to that bathroom, I cried. I started saying to myself, "God I don't know what to do." It was like I was praying unintentionally. At that moment, a young lady came into the bathroom and saw me standing by the mirror.

She said, "Hi Porchia! I know you don't remember me, but I was at the school when you were running for campus queen. I saw that you graduated and moved to L.A. You inspired me so much!" I was taken aback by her greeting, but I said hi and kept talking with her as she asked me a few questions about L.A. Then she said, "Keep following your dreams and doing what you're doing because you got people out here like me that's watching you." I think I hugged her at that moment. She had no clue what her words had done for me. Just when

I was contemplating my decisions, I believe God sent her at that moment to let me know I am in alignment with what He is doing in my life. I needed that affirmation more than she knew.

I got myself together, put back on a smile, and confidently walked out of that bathroom. When I returned to the reception hall, everyone was on the dance floor. I joined in and had a great time. The issue was that those wine refills caught up to me. I was absolutely drunk by the time I left that wedding. I hadn't eaten much food and had approximately 5 to 7 glasses of wine. Since I hadn't drank any alcoholic beverages in a while, it was easy for it to affect me in that way, I guess. The former line sister I was lodging with at that time took me to get food because I was puking on the way back to our hotel. I even tried to go out with them that night and didn't even make it out of the car.

I share that story to let you know you have to be bold in this transition. You have to stand on the truth of God's word. My lack of boldness led me to the sin of drunkenness. I was emotional, discouraged, and got into my feelings rather than letting the truth speak for me. People will come for you in this transition. They will say all kinds of things to make you feel bad. Most of the people who try to confront you or talk bad about you won't understand because they chose to walk in darkness. You have to trust God and stand on His word regardless of what other people may think of you.

In the previous chapter, I spoke about how I eventually had the Zoom call with the whole line. This was a month or so after this fiasco. I was slightly nervous because of the few interactions I had already had. However, I needed to finally denounce the organization to the people who mattered most in this situation. Not everyone joined the call, but those who did listened to me. I spoke with the boldness of what God had revealed to me. And to my surprise, they all showed me love. They let me know that they supported my decision and wouldn't treat me with contempt because of it. That was a weight lifted off of my shoulders.

Not everyone will be in full support of your decision to renounce and denounce the secret societies and ungodly organizations you depart from. That doesn't mean you shrink back and hide. Just like I was surprised by the love shown to me, you may be surprised by who supports you as you navigate this new journey of freedom! You can do it. I am rooting for you.

Here are some GPS Checkpoints for navigating the transition of being free from secret societies:

1 Always remain prayerful! The Bible tells us to pray without ceasing for a reason. We can not go through this life and its changes without being in communication with God. (see 1 Thessalonians 5:17)

2 Tell whoever needs to know, regardless of what you think they may say.

   - People may think you are crazy or over-exaggerating, but that is on them, not you.

   - It can be a challenge trying to explain spiritual things to carnal people. However, it is not your job to persuade anyone to make any decisions they are not ready for. Plant the seeds of truth and keep it moving.

3. Ignore all negative feedback from family, friends and social media platforms.

   - Forgive these people quickly! They have no clue what they are saying, or who they are coming up against. You are backed by God when you are obedient to Him, so you have nothing to worry about.

- ❧ Meditate on Isaiah 54:15-17.
4. Seek counseling or therapy if you feel led by God to do so.

    - ❧ There is a level of grieving that comes with this transition. Pray and ask God to help you in this area.

    - ❧ If God tells you to seek Godly counsel regarding this, don't shy away from it. Talk to who He leads you to.
5. Pray and ask God to send you someone who can pray with you along this journey.

    - ❧ God sent my friend Jasmine. She has prayed with me, fasted with me, and spiritually went to war on my behalf throughout this journey.

6. Don't Judge Anyone!

- ❧ Friends, family and people that you meet who are still in these secret societies are also loved by God. Whether they repent and obey Him or not has nothing to do with you.

- ❧ Don't participate in the things God has called you out of with them; also, don't make them feel like they're beneath you. We are not better than anyone just because we answered God's call.

- ❧ Love everyone deeply as the Bible tells us to in 1 Peter 4:8.

Lastly, I want to share with you this scripture:

> *Am I now trying to win the approval of human beings, or of God? Or am I trying to please people? If I were still trying to please people, I would not be a servant of Christ."* - **Galatians 1:10 NIV**

This is the scripture that helped me walk in obedience to do what God has called me to do in sharing this message. Fear of people would make me a people pleaser. If I am a people pleaser, doing only what other people want me to do, then that means I am not pleasing God. If someone has more say or control over what I should do than God has, then that is another level of idolatry. We must do what God tells us to do no matter what people think or say.

Had I listened to the person who told me not to make a YouTube video of public denouncement, then I would still be bound. Furthermore, pleasing people removes me from being a servant of Jesus Christ. God has way too many promises for His servants for me to revoke my position as a servant.

For instance, Exodus 23:25-26 says, *"So you shall serve the LORD your God, and He will bless your bread and your water. And I will take sickness away from the midst of you. No one shall suffer miscarriage or be barren in your land; I will fulfill the number of your days."* This is an amazing promise that God has for people who serve Him (His servants). No one's thoughts or opinions of what I am doing for God has enough persuasion to make me forfeit my promises as a servant. You should have that same viewpoint. Fear God, not man. Please God, not people.

5

HOW TO FIGHT THIS FIGHT

Self Defense VS God's Defense

There is a celebration in heaven and on earth for your newfound freedom in God! However, coming out from among them will not go without a fight. Spiritual warfare will be at an all-time high. The enemies of your soul will try to attack you on every end. The blessing in this is that when you fight, you fight from a place of victory through prayer.

The interesting thing about spiritual warfare is that we are never fighting against the flesh and blood that seemingly comes against us. This is revealed in Ephesians 6:12. There is always a spiritual force at work in conflict. We are spiritual beings living a human experience. Therefore, what we see in the natural is not as real as what is seen in the spiritual. Due to the highly spiritual nature of the enemies we have, we must fight them in our highest spiritual action, which is prayer.

When we pray, we must pray the word of God! The word of God defeats these enemies. We see the evidence of that in Luke 4:2-13 when Jesus defeated Satan in the wilderness with the word of God. His words are powerful. In Hebrews 4:12 it says, "For the word of God is living and powerful, and sharper than any two-edged sword, piercing even to the division of soul and spirit, and of joints and marrow, and is a discerner of the thoughts and intents of the heart." There is nothing more powerful in the world than God's word. God actually showed me that in a dream where I had to use his word to defeat an enemy.

Here's what happened in that dream...

I was in an apartment, ironically, with a few former line sisters. A guy named Christian showed up to the gathering we were having. Christian got very angry with me for some reason, and we started arguing. He turned into a demonic-looking angry man, chasing me down a hallway with a gun. He got close to me and tried to grab me, and somehow, in that interaction, he ended up on the floor. His gun fell out of his hand and slid across the hallway floor.

I picked up my phone and called the police. I told them a man was chasing me with a gun, trying to kill me. His gun is now on the floor and he is about to get back up. I told them if they don't hurry up and come, then I will have to use self-defense and shoot this man with his own gun. The dispatcher on the phone was saying she understood, when a man came out of nowhere, shot and killed the man who was trying to get back up and get to me.

While I was screaming at what was happening, he took the gun and shot me in the foot. I started crying and yelling at him. I told him how I was the victim and that man was trying to kill me. Then I said, "I thought you were trying to help me, so why would you shoot me in my foot?" He said, "because you said you had to use self defense. I want the scene to look believable when the police get here." I was so confused, but I ended up waking up briefly and then went back to sleep.

When I went back to sleep, the dream started over. Everything that happened before the chasing was happening, only this time, I didn't argue with Christian when he got upset with me out of nowhere. I already knew where the dream was headed, so I just started running down the hallway again.

I turned the corner to my left and ran right into an open door. It was an apartment with some guy sitting at a piano with headphones on and playing his music. I asked him if I could go hide in his room. He said yes. I ran in there and found a closet to hide in.

Then I heard the evil guy chasing me enter the apartment. I think he may have gotten rid of the guy that was out there at the piano, so I knew he couldn't save me. I heard his footsteps come into the room and my heart dropped to the pit of my stomach. I was so scared I wanted to hold my breath so that he couldn't hear me breathe.

To my surprise, courage rose up in me all of a sudden. I felt bold enough to get out of the closet and fight because I didn't want him to start shooting while I was in there. I came out of the closet, stepped into the middle of the room facing him. The gun was pointed directly at my face, and I could see down the barrel of it. I looked at him and I said, "No weapon formed against me shall prosper."

Just then, the gun fell out of his hand and his arms twisted backward. I couldn't believe what I was seeing. But it got me excited, so I said, "Oh you like that huh?" Then I said the scripture again. He then fell on the bed that was next to us on the left. I remember quoting "greater is He that is within me" at some point. And his whole body changed dark and he began shriveling up. I kept quoting those two scriptures that I could remember and by the time I was done, he was dead.

When I woke up from that dream, I just knew God had given me the secret sauce to winning these spiritual wars. I know that dream had a lot of interpretation and things that needed to be unpacked; however, what I took from it was me defeating a demon with God's word. This is how I learned to pray the scriptures. God made it clear to me that self-defense doesn't work in the spirit realm. There is no flesh and blood to fight with there. God's defense is His word. Ephesians 6:17 lets us know that the sword of The Spirit is the word of God. It is also the only weapon we have to fight with in the spiritual armor mentioned from verses 10 through 17 of that passage.

When we attempt to defend ourselves, we want every possible weapon we can think of. With God's defense, there is only one weapon required. Self-defense also puts us in control of a situation, while God's defense gives Him full control to handle it all. In self-defense, we tend to fight people with our words, while God's defense uses His word, which always prevails. Our wins are not always guaranteed with self-defense, but with God's defense we have guaranteed victory always.

I want you to be encouraged that you are victorious. When you read, study, meditate and apply God's word to your life, there isn't too much Satan can do to you. Yes he will try to send afflictions. However, Psalms 34:19 promises us that God will deliver us from all affliction. No matter what kind of fight you encounter while getting free from these secret societies, please know that in the end, you will win! There is nothing that anyone can say or do to stop your victory in Christ Jesus. There is no weapon that the enemy can try to throw at your life that will take you out. Trust God and His word always.

<u>Here are a few of my favorite spiritual warfare scriptures that I want you to look up, read, memorize and pray with...</u>

Isaiah54:15-17; Luke10:19; Psalms27:2-3; Psalms35:1; 2Corinthians10:3-5; Deuteronomy 20:4; Jeremiah1:19; Psalms44:7; Exodus14:14; 2Timothy1:7; Deuteronomy 3:22; Psalms 60:12; 1John4:4; Matthew16:19; Romans8:37; Ephesians6:10-20; Psalms91;
1Corinthians15:57; Psalms124: 6-8

CONCLUSION

True Identity in Christ

These secret societies always take you away from your true identity in Christ. They suppress who you really are in God and make you behave in a way that is opposite to who God has called you to be. There is a spirit behind each organization that draws out insecurities and certain personality types of certain individuals. For instance, if you are considered a "pretty girl" then you would most likely want to be a part of the AKA sorority. Or if you are a prideful man, you would want to be an Alpha. The list can go on to include how people with tough exteriors join particular organizations, and how people who suffer from the spirit of rejection join the organizations that seem lesser than the bigger ones.

Some people take on personas and viewpoints that don't even matter to them for the sake of these organizations. I remember at some point I couldn't stand seeing the colors pink and green together all because I was a Delta. That mindset made me feel

CONCLUSION

like I was somehow better than women who chose the sorority those colors are attributed to. That is just one of many examples I can give of how people easily get their identities wrapped up in things God doesn't even have for them.

If you have made it to the end of this book, and are in one of these secret societies, ask God to show you who you really are. Ask Him to reveal to you what He thinks about these organizations. The revelation manifests itself in different ways. For me, it happened because I was tired of having horrible dreams and nightmares. For others it may have been an encounter, a book or YouTube video that revealed the truth. Nevertheless, when you have decided to take your relationship with God to the next level, allow Him to speak with you about everything. Don't shut off this part of your life to Him.

God wants all of you. All of you should be a reflection to Him. He has given us a plethora of scripture that speaks to the truth of who we are. He has laid the foundation of the type of character we are supposed to have and the personality we should embrace. Our character should be a Christ-like character, and not the character of a particular organization. How we behave, our mindsets, our viewpoints and so forth should come from what He has shared with us in His word and through spending quality time with Him. If your whole identity is based on the organization you are a part of, that is an issue that needs to be addressed in prayer.

In conclusion, my earnest prayer is that this book has been a source of enlightenment and transformation for you. I hope it has stirred a deep desire within you to delve even further into the Word of God and to ignite your prayer life to new heights.

Throughout your journey with this book, I trust that you've gained a profound understanding of what God's Word reveals about secret societies. Remember that when you seek God on any topic, you always find Him.

As you continue to seek God in all aspects of your life, know this: He is everything you need. Your identity in Christ is not only sufficient but also more than enough to propel you to success in this life. You do not require the endorsement of any secret society to wield influence or make a lasting impact on the world. You do not need a secret society to define who you are. In the grand scheme of things, it is only what God says about you that truly matters.

So, people of God, seize hold of this truth and run with it relentlessly, for in Christ, you are a chosen generation, a royal priesthood, a holy nation, and His own special person—called out of darkness into His marvelous light. Embrace your identity in Christ, and you will navigate life's journey with unwavering purpose and unshakeable confidence.

May God's grace and peace accompany you on your continued walk with Him.

> *"But you are a chosen generation, a royal priesthood, a holy nation, His own special people, that you may proclaim the praises of Him who called you out of darkness into His marvelous light;"* - 1 Peter 2:9

ACKNOWLEDGEMENTS

To **Minister Kevin LA Ewing**. Thank You!!! You have played a major role in helping me understand spiritual principles in the Bible. During the challenging times of the world shutdown in 2020, your teachings provided me with profound insights and helped me walk into the light of truth concerning the things discussed in this book. Thank you for your boldness, for defying all odds, and for encouraging God's people with His transformative word. Your dedication to spreading the message of faith and hope has been a source of inspiration.

ABOUT THE AUTHOR

Porchia Carter is a dynamic author, media personality, and visionary entrepreneur who boldly and joyfully shares her unwavering faith with the world. Born and raised in the vibrant city of Detroit, Michigan, she currently resides in the bustling metropolis of New York. She is the CEO and founder of Porchia Carter Enterprises LLC, a media company producing content that edifies the soul. Porchia's multifaceted talents extend beyond the realm of the writing. She is a captivating performing artist, proficient in acting, dance, and hosting. With passion and purpose, she utilizes her artistic gifts to spread the boundless joy of the Lord to everyone she encounters. Porchia Carter is not only an author but also a best-selling one, having penned her first book, "*All Things Work Together*," which has touched the hearts and minds of many readers.

www.ingramcontent.com/pod-product-compliance
Lightning Source LLC
Chambersburg PA
CBHW050656160426
43194CB00010B/1956